Other Books By Felix Harder

Click On The Cover To Go To The Book

TABLE OF CONTENTS

Introduction

Getting a six-pack is high on everybody's list of fitness goals. Poll after poll has shown that wanting to build their abdominal muscles is what brings most men into the gym. At the same time, it's the muscle group that women find the most attractive in men.

Unfortunately, due to all the hype around six-pack / abdominal training, there is a lot of misguiding information out there. Infomercial workout equipment and most fat loss pills are a complete waste of your money and time. Even if they might promise it, no product is going to magically make your mid-section more muscular and your abs more toned.

Great abs require a great workout. This workout doesn't have to be hours long, it just has to hit the right muscles with the right amount of repetitions. Additionally, you need the right diet and supplements. That's where this book comes into play. It's going to cover all these aspects and more. We will start with the anatomy of the ab muscles. You will see that not all muscles are created equal and they need different training.

The second part of the book covers the best workout routines you should be doing for optimal muscle growth. I listed every exercise and the *exact* amount of reps you should be doing. Part three is all about nutrition and supplements. You probably know that the right foods are even more important than the right training. But what exactly should you eat, and what supplements do you need? Don't worry, I've got you covered.

At the end of the book I included a list of the best ab exercises. Each exercise is explained in detail, with a picture, safety tips and possible variations. That way you will never have to worry about finding new exercises when working out your core.

- Felix Harder

Abdominal Muscles Anatomy

In order to develop great abs, you need to understand the basic anatomy of all the different muscles involved. This includes their functions and specific location. Only when you know how each muscle works, can you train them properly. Of course, you don't need to remember every last detail about muscle anatomy. To train effectively, focus on understanding where the abdominal muscles are located and what their exact functions are.

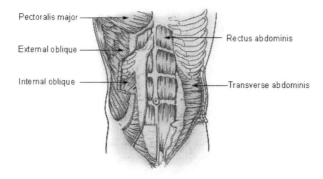

Your core is made up of several different muscles. On the anterior core those are:

- The three muscle groups of the deep layer (thoracic diaphragm, pelvic floor, transverse abdominis). They help pressurize your inner-core musculature, which is important for heavy exercises such as squats or deadlifts.

- The intermediate layer with its most important muscle, the internal oblique, which helps with respiration and torso rotation.

- The superficial layer which includes the external oblique and the rectus abdominus. These are the muscles you mean when talking about a six-pack.

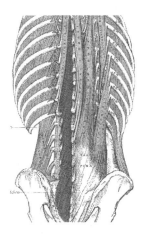

Next to the muscles on the anterior core, there are three important muscles on the posterior core (see picture above):

- The multifidus, which helps control small movements throughout your spine

- The quadratus lumborum, which is important for controlling the different motions in your core.

- The erector spinae, a subgroup of muscles dedicated to straightening the back.

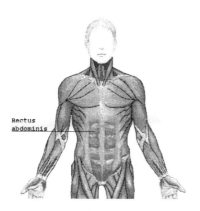

Most important facts:

- The rectus abdominis is a sheet of muscle, which runs laterally from sternum to pelvis.

- Is visible from the outside and usually referred to as the six-pack muscle.

- The number of packs your abs show is determined by the number of connective tissues crossing your abdominal region (called bands of fascia).

Detailed explanation:

The rectus abdominus muscle originates (starts) at the bottom of the sternum and inserts (ends) at the pelvis into the fifth, sixth, and seventh ribs. Its main function is to pull your knees up to your torso, increase abdominal pressure, and stabilize the pelvis. When we speak about training the upper or lower abs, you should keep in mind, that they are part of the same muscle group and simply two different ends of it.

Training:

The basic exercises to train the rectus abdominus muscle are crunches and sit-ups. There are literally hundreds of variations to these two traditional exercises, which will affect how the muscle is working. Static or non-movement contractions like the plank can also be used to strengthen your rectus abdominis.

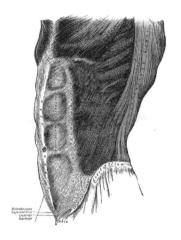

Most important facts:

- The external obliques run diagonally down the sides of your body toward the midline of the body.

- Are visible from the outside and provide the "V" shape that frame the lower abs.

- Twists the body from side to side.

Detailed explanation:

The external obliques originate on the lower eight ribs and run down to your hips, where they insert at the lower part of your pubic area. They have parallel-orientated fibers that form a flat muscle architecture. This muscle group gives the torso a more detailed look that many well-conditioned athletes and bodybuilders are famous for. The external obliques act as a trunk flexor and rotator, but also play a crucial role in muscle stability within the core and midsection. Strong external obliques are necessary for any exercise that requires lateral stabilization.

Training:

The external obliques are engaged in almost every compound lifting movement, but can also be trained with certain isolation movements. Possible exercises include side crunches, dumbbell side bends, knee raises to your sides and medicine ball twists.

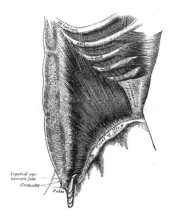

Most important facts:

- Lie below the external obliques and run in the opposite direction.

- Serve a similar purpose as external obliques.

Detailed explanation:

The internal obliques lie as a flat sheet of muscle below the external obliques. The muscle originates at the middle of your anterior trunk and inserts at around the hip bone. Next to its function as a torso rotator, it compresses the abdomen and helps with respiration. The external and internal obliques are collectively referred to as the "obliques". Together they carry out the same movements, however, the internal obliques act as same-side rotators, while the external obliques are opposite-side rotators.

<u>Training:</u>

See External Obliques

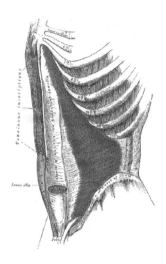

Most important facts:

- The transverse abdominis is the deepest muscle of the abdominal wall.

- Reduces the diameter of the abdomen.

- Invisible to the eye.

Detailed explanation:

The transverse abdominus lies directly below the rectus abdominus and is the deepest layer of muscle in the abdominal wall. It originates along the hip bone and on the lower six ribs and inserts into the lower part of your pubic area. The muscle acts as a natural belt and keeps organs from distending out past the ribcage and stabilizes the lumbar spine.

Training:

Isolating the transverse abdominus is difficult, which is why you should train the muscle indirectly. Good exercises for this include side planks and side bridges. This way, you will improve and strengthen the transverse abdominus, while also working other abdominal muscles.

The Perfect Workout

There are countless theories out there about how to best train abs. As confusing as they might be for beginners, all of them lie between two extreme workout routines:

- A long and hard ab workout done about once a week, just like you would do for any other muscle group.

- A short ab workout done daily or every other day.

So what's the better of the two?
And what exercises should I do?
And how many sets / reps?

We will answer all of these questions in a bit. For now, let us look at a mistake many new lifters make when selecting an ab workout. They fail to realize that they already train their abs several times per week, even when not doing any direct ab exercises. Almost every compound movement - such as in the traditional deadlift - involves your core and therefore your abs. That is why some guys can get away with no special ab workout at all and still have a great six-pack. I will suppose that you are not part of this tiny group of gifted men. For the vast majority of us, compound exercises alone are not enough to stimulate significant muscle growth in the abs. But don't worry! With the right workout and a little work you'll be part of the six-pack club in no more than four to six weeks.

Another common mistake is thinking that ab muscles are any different from the other muscles in our body. Proponents of this theory tend to think that since the abs are smaller, they need less time to recover. However, there is no scientific proof for this and any doctor will tell you that your ab muscles really aren't chemically different from your other muscles. All of them are composed of muscle fiber tissues and will respond in similar ways. No matter what part of your body, muscle growth (= muscle hypertrophy) is always achieved through the same process.

After a workout, the body repairs damaged muscle fibers through a cellular process where muscle fibers are fused together to form new muscle protein strands (=myofibrils). The repaired muscle strands increase in number and thickness, which leads to muscle growth. This growth, however, does not occur while lifting the weights. Instead, it happens while you rest. The harder you work your muscles, the more damage you will do and, therefore, the more rest you will need.

Assuming you are doing productive abdominal workouts, there is no additional benefit to training abs every single day. In fact, it will hurt your muscle growth, because your muscles won't have sufficient time to rest in between the workouts.

There are countless ab exercises you could do, but that doesn't mean you should do them. Most of them target the rectus abdominis and the obliques, the two most visible core muscles. In order to force these two muscle groups to grow, you will have to add weighted exercises to your repertoire. Crunches and sit-ups simply don't offer enough resistance to cause much muscle hypertrophy. That's the reason you can do so many of them; by themselves they are too easy! Only when you combine them with more difficult (=weighted) exercises, will you be able to really work the rectus abdominis and the obliques. I will show you what weighted exercises work best in the workout plan.

As you already know, the rectus abdominis and the obliques make up only part of your trunk. If you want to develop a strong core, you should also include certain other exercises in your normal workout routine. These exercises don't have to be done in conjunction with your ab workout, since most of them are compound exercises and fit better into your back and/or chest day:

- Deadlifts
- Military Press
- Hyperextensions
- Squats

This is a great question that always causes a lot of debate among bodybuilders. Should you do high-rep, low intensity ab training or low-rep, high intensity ab training? As you might know from my other books, I am a big fan of heavy training and a low rep count. In the case of ab training this goes against many traditional workout routines, which advise dozens or even hundreds of crunches a set. The problem with this approach is simple. As you increase reps, you will reach a certain point where more reps don't equal more gains. You will not be building muscle strength but endurance. This point is reached very early, in weighted ab exercises as low as 12 reps per set. Research actually confirms this, as it has been proven that the growth you see during lighter lifting involving more reps is due partly to an increase in the volume of the fluid in your muscle (water, glycogen, etc.) and it will disappear after a few days of rest. Heavier lifting and fewer reps on the other hand, always lead to an actual increase in the size of the muscle fibers.

In this workout plan you will train abs twice a week at the end of your normal workout routine. So if you are doing a 3-day split and usually train on Monday, Wednesday and Friday, you should add this ab workout on Monday and Friday.

Monday – Day 1 + Abs

Tuesday – Rest

Wednesday – Day 2

Thursday – Rest

Friday – Day 3 + Abs

Saturday – Rest

Sunday – Rest

Never train your abs first, as they are part of your core area and help stabilize your body. If you fatigue them early in your workout, you will suffer during other ab-intensive exercises like squats. As said before, you will see the best results if you do weighted exercises and un-weighted exercises. When doing weighted exercises, try to work with heavy weights. When doing un-weighted, go to failure. You will feel the results on the day after, I promise.

Before each workout:

Be sure to eat plenty of carbohydrates so your body can lift at maximum strength. Your last meal should be maximum 1.5 - 2 hours before your training session.

Warm Up:

Warm ups are a good way to prevent injuries and help the muscle perform at its maximum. The increased blood flow will also keep your muscles sustained with nutrients. Before your first exercise, you should also do a warm up set (10 repetitions) with light weight to warm up the specific muscle group.

Note: You can find a detailed description of every exercise at the end of the book under "All Ab Exercises."

Day 1

1. Exercise: Cable Crunch

1 Warm-Up Set of 10 – 12 Reps
3 Working Sets of 10 – 12 Reps

2. Exercise: Hanging Leg Raises

3 Working Sets of 10 – 12 Reps (possible with a dumbbell in between your feet)

3. Exercise: Twisting Crunch

3 Working Sets of 10 – 12 Reps (or until failure)

Day 2

1. Exercise: Cable Crunch

1 Warm-Up Set of 10 – 12 Reps
3 Working Sets of 10 – 12 Reps

2. Exercise: Decline Cross Crunch

3 Working Sets of 10 – 12 Reps (or until failure)

3. Exercise: Ab Rollout On Knees

3 Working Sets of 10 – 12 Reps (or until failure)

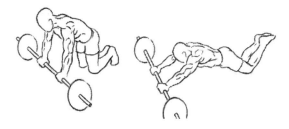

In this workout plan, you will train abs three times a week at the end of your normal workout routine. So if you are doing a 3-day split and usually train on Monday, Wednesday and Friday, you should add this ab workout on all three days.

Monday – Day 1 + Abs

Tuesday – Rest

Wednesday – Day 2 + Abs

Thursday – Rest

Friday – Day 3 + Abs

Saturday – Rest

Sunday – Rest

This advanced workout is meant for experienced trainees looking for exercises to really get the most out of their ab days. Your muscles have already gotten used to lifting heavier weights and now is the time to step it up a little to see some serious results. When going through this workout routine, pay close attention to your rectus abdominis and obliques to make sure you don't over train them. As before, try to work with heavy weights when doing weighted exercises and go to failure during un-weighted exercises.

Before each workout:

Be sure to eat plenty of carbohydrates so your body can lift at maximum strength.

Your last meal should be maximum 1.5 - 2 hours before your training session.

Warm Up:

Warm ups are a good way to prevent injuries and help the muscle perform at its maximum. The increased blood flow will also keep your muscles sustained with nutrients. Before your first exercise you should also do a warm up set (10 repetitions) with light weight to warm up the specific muscle group.

Note: You can find a detailed description of every exercise at the end of the book under "All Ab Exercises."

Day 1

1. Exercise: Cable Crunch

1 Warm-Up Set of 10 – 12 Reps
3 Working Sets of 10 – 12 Reps

2. Exercise: Ab Rollout On Knees

3 Working Sets of 10 – 12 Reps (or until failure)

3. Exercise: Twisting Crunch

3 Working Sets of 10 – 12 Reps (or until failure)

Day 2

1. Exercise: <u>Hanging Leg Raises</u> (with a dumbbell in between your feet)

1 Warm-Up Set of 10 – 12 Reps
3 Working Sets of 10 – 12 Reps

2. Exercise: <u>Decline Crunch</u>

3 Working Sets of 10 – 12 Reps (or until failure)

3. Exercise: Decline Cross Crunch

3 Working Sets of 10 – 12 Reps (or until failure)

Day 3

1. Exercise: Cable Crunch

1 Warm-Up Set of 10 – 12 Reps
3 Working Sets of 10 – 12 Reps

2. Exercise: Dumbbell Side Bends

3 Working Sets of 10 – 12 Reps (or until failure)

3. Exercise: Twisting Crunch

3 Working Sets of 10 – 12 Reps (or until failure)

Even though most of us don't like to admit it, cardio can be just as important for a great six-pack as the right exercises. It all depends on your body fat percentage. Even if you didn't train your abs at all, they would still show if you have a low body fat percentage. Your abs will most likely look flat and not "pop," but they will be more impressive than that gym-gut many lifters have.

In their case the ab muscles are hidden by layers of fat. More ab exercises most likely won't do the trick for them. Unless they lose the extra fat, their abs will always stay invisible. So how can you bring your body fat percentage down?

Unfortunately, losing body fat is not the easiest of propositions. Many beginners give up their training entirely, because they can't seem to get rid of these ten or twenty pounds that keep them from having their dream six-pack. That will not happen to you! Interestingly, the most effective fat loss method does not involve running a marathon every day.

Instead you need a combination of weight training, light but regular cardio and the right diet. We already covered the weight training part, now you need to know *when* and *how long* to do cardio.

There are two times of the day you can do your cardio, directly after your normal workout or first thing in the morning. Both will stimulate greater gains in fat loss because your glycogen stores will be depleted at this time and therefore fat will be burned directly for fuel. Beginners should never do their cardio before a workout because of lesser strength and energy. They would use up the body's preferred energy source (= glycogen) for the cardio instead of the weight training. This can be dangerous when lifting heavy weights for example, during compound exercises.

Another drawback of completing cardio first, is the release of cortisol without a parallel increase in testosterone. Cortisol breaks down muscle in order to provide your body the needed energy to work out. This works fine when doing cardiovascular exercises and occurs extensively in long duration cardio (like marathons), but is disadvantageous to building muscle if there's not a simultaneous increase in testosterone.

If you want to get the most out of your cardio sessions, there are three variables that you should know and pay attention to: Intensity, Duration and Frequency.

- Intensity describes the percentage of your maximum heart rate that you use when performing a particular exercise.

- Duration refers to how long each session will last.

- Frequency refers to how often you do cardio during a certain time interval (e.g. one week)

These three variables can be combined in different ways, each producing a different end result. As a rule of thumb, one can say that high intensity sessions and a shorter duration will help improve your cardiovascular system, but are not the best method for burning fat. For that your will have to combine a medium intensity session with a longer duration. Lastly, frequency will depend on your personal goals and needs. Let's have a more detailed look at the three variables.

Intensity:

All cardiovascular exercise can be categorized into three major groups of intensity: mild, moderate and high. Mild intensity would equal an easy walking pace, while moderate is what most people think when talking about cardio. High intensity is reached once you are no longer able to talk during the exercise. For optimal fat burning, most studies suggest moderate intensity workout. This assures that between 85 - 90% of calories burned are fat calories (instead of glucose).

If you increase the intensity, this rate will drop and your body will start using more glucose. Once your body is working so hard that the demands for fuel and oxygen exceed the rate of supply, more and more glucose is broken down or metabolized into a substance called pyruvate. This process produces a byproduct known as lactic acid, which you want to avoid by any means, because it hurts your muscle growth.

How can you make sure to stay in the optimal fat burning window? It's actually easier than you might think. To efficiently burn fat in the shortest amount of time, you need to do moderate cardio with your heart rate at 65%-75% of your maximum heart rate. Because most of us don't have a heart rate monitor next to us when running on the treadmill, try to find the pace that lies just between being able to talk and being able to sing. If you are able to both talk and sing, your heart rate will most likely be below 65%, but if you can neither talk nor sing, you are already doing high intensity cardio above 75% of your maximum heart rate. This trick might seems a bit silly, but it has worked for bodybuilders and athletes for decades.

Duration:

How long should my cardio session last? If you want to see real results, your sessions will have to last at least 20 minutes. Only then will your body have used up most of its instantaneous energy sources and will have to find other ways of providing your body with energy. Now your body will start tapping into your stored body fat to allow your body to continue at the same intensity. Once you reach 30 minutes at your optimal heart rate, your body will be burning an even larger percentage of calories from fat. Nevertheless, I wouldn't suggest you do more than 45 minutes of cardio each session. Even if you have a lot of extra fat you want to lose, it doesn't make sense to stay on the treadmill for hours and hours. Most people don't particularly enjoy cardio and it will be hard to keep this routine up when you also have three or more workout sessions a week.

Frequency:

How often you do cardio really depends on your goals and needs. I always recommend starting small with two or three 20-minute sessions per week. If you just got into bodybuilding, then it is better to take it slowly instead of trying the Arnold Schwarzenegger routine in your first week. The key is to be persistent, not to train like a maniac one week and skip two sessions the next. Once you have gained some experience but still feel like you need to lose a few pounds, you can increase cardio frequency to three, four or even more times per week. This will allow your body to adjust to the additional stress and work it is being put through instead of slamming into it.

Nutrition and Supplements

You have probably heard that the right nutrition is more important than the right workout. Well, it's true. If you don't give your muscles the necessary tools for a proper recovery and growth, then they won't get bigger or stronger. As all bodybuilders know, you will never see any significant gains if you aren't eating sufficient amounts of high quality food. Nutrition is about providing nourishment to your body. The human body needs proper nourishment for the maintenance of our body (muscles, bone, tissues, etc.) and muscle growth. So how do you provide your body with proper nutrition?

That's what macronutrients and micronutrients are for. Macronutrients make up the majority of your diet. The most important macronutrients are carbohydrates, protein, fat and water. Carbs, fats and proteins are interchangeable as sources of energy, with fats yielding nine calories per gram, and protein and carbohydrates both yielding four calories per gram.

Micronutrients are vitamins and trace minerals. They are called micronutrients because your body only requires them in very small amounts. Vitamins are organic substances that we ingest with our foods, which act like catalysts, substances that help to trigger other reactions in the body. Trace minerals are inorganic substances which play a role in several metabolic processes, and contribute to the synthesis of such elements as protein, glycogen and fats.

Carbohydrates ("carbs"):

Despite what many people want you to believe, carbs are not evil. They are an important source of energy for your body. The problem is that the average person over-consumes certain sources of carbohydrates, usually simple sugars from candy and soda, while forgetting about the complex carbs found in brown rice, sweet potatoes and oats. These are especially important for bodybuilders, since you need to make sure to cover your daily calorie requirements through healthy foods, which your body can actually process.

Good Sources of Carbohydrate:

- Vegetables (all kinds)
- Fruit
- Oats and oatmeal
- Brown Rice
- Seeds
- Nuts
- Quinoa
- Chia
- Yams
- Lentils
- Whole Grain Breads
- Whole Grain Pitas
- Whole Grain Cereals
- (Sweet) Potatoes
- Whole grain pastas

- Beans

Carbohydrates to limit or avoid:

- White Pasta
- White Rice
- White Bread
- Instant Oatmeal
- Fruit Juices
- Bagels
- Donuts
- Muffins
- Sweets and Candies
- Processed Breakfast Cereals
- Processed corn products
- Processed potato products
- Processed rice products

Proteins:

Protein is a linked chain of amino acids, necessary for your body to maintain, grow and repair damage to its muscles. The normal adult gets enough protein through a healthy diet of natural foods, though an intense exercise program like the one in this book will call for a higher protein intake and the use of protein shakes for optimal results.

There are various myths about protein shakes, such as that they are bad for your kidneys. While there might have been a few cases of kidney problems due to the excessive use of protein supplements, all you need to do to avoid this problem is drink more water. Excess protein will be flushed out of your kidneys and you will simply pee it out. Another popular discussion in the bodybuilding scene regards the amount of protein you need to consume in order to build muscle. Research has shown that the average trainee looking to build muscle should consume between 0.6g and 1.1g of protein per pound of bodyweight. The exact amount depends on your genetics, goals and the rest of your diet, but you should aim to hit somewhere in that range.

Good Sources of Protein:

- Fish (Tuna, Salmon, Halibut)
- Lean Chicken (Chicken Breast)
- Cheese (Non-fat Mozzarella)
- Lean Beef and Veal (Low Fat)
- Pork Loin (Chops)
- Yogurt, Milk, and Soymilk
- Beans (Mature Soy Beans)
- Eggs (Especially Egg Whites)
- Nuts and Seeds (Pumpkin, Squash, and Watermelon Seeds)

Disclaimer: Animal products such as meat, eggs and dairy are good sources of protein; however, they can also be high in saturated fat and cholesterol. That is why more and more bodybuilders switch to a vegetarian or even vegan diet. Here are a few good vegetarian and vegan sources of protein:

- Green peas
- Quinoa
- Nuts and nut butter
- Beans
- Chickpeas
- Tempeh and Tofu
- Edamame
- Leafy greens
- Hemp

Fats:

Just like calories, fats are not evil, per se. Instead, they perform a variety of necessary functions in your body. The problem is that most people eat too many saturated fats and trans fats, which increase LDL ("bad") cholesterol and decrease HDL ("good") cholesterol, while eating too few healthy fats like monounsaturated fats (found in canola oil and olive oil) and Omega-3 fatty acids (found in flax seed oil, fish and other sources). A diet, which includes healthy fats, will help you pack on muscle much quicker than any low fat diet.

Good Sources of Healthy Fats:

- Avocados
- Eggs
- Olive Oil
- Nuts
- Nut Butter
- Fatty Fish
- Dark Chocolate (in moderate amounts)
- Coconuts and Coconut Oil

Fatty Foods to limit or avoid:

- Pizza
- Burgers
- Microwaved Popcorn
- French Fries
- Frozen Foods

- Cookies
- Potato Chips

In bodybuilding there are two important phases, the bulking and the cutting phase. Bulking is done primarily to gain size and strength, while the goal of cutting is to lower your body fat percentage and achieving that more toned look. Bodybuilders usually alternate the two phases, because it allows them to gain muscle faster during the bulking phase and to lose extra fat afterwards during the cutting phase.

A proper six pack meal plan falls into the cutting phase, where you want to consume less calories than you burn, in order to lose fat and make the muscles pop. That is why the following meal plan will be high in protein (65-70%) and low in carbs (15-20%) and fat (5-10%).

Day 1

Breakfast (around 550 calories):

- 6 egg whites (100-135 calories)
- 1 tbsp. Peanut butter (180 calories)
- 1 serving of steel cut oats (100-150 calories)
- 1 scoop of whey protein (120 calories)

Midmorning Snack (around 190 calories)

- 1 can of tuna (low sodium) (100 calories)
- 1 Greek Yogurt (fat free) (80-100 calories)

Lunch (around 450 calories)

- 8 oz. chicken or white fish (240 calories)
- 1 sweet potato (150 calories)
- 2-3 servings of vegetables (50-75 calories)

Afternoon Snack and Post Workout (around 180 calories)

- 1 scoop of whey protein (120 calories)
- 1 medium sized banana (60 calories)

Dinner (around 600 calories)

- 2 servings of lean venison or lamb (500-600 calories)
- 3 servings vegetables (50-75 calories)

Evening Snack (around 270 calories)

- 1 serving steel cut oats (100-150 calories)
- ½ tbsp. Peanut butter (95-100 calories)
- 1 medium sized banana (60 calories)

Day 2

Breakfast (around 550 calories):

- 6 egg whites (100-135 calories)
- 1 tbsp. Peanut butter (180 calories)
- 1 serving of steel cut oats (100-150 calories)
- 1 scoop of whey protein (120 calories)

Midmorning Snack (around 280 calories)

- 1 serving of organic cereal with ½ serving plain almond milk (125-150 calories)
- 1 medium sized banana (60 calories)
- 1 fat free Greek Yogurt (80-100 calories)

Lunch (around 450 calories)

- 8 oz. fat free ground turkey (240 calories)
- 2-3 servings of vegetables (50-75 calories)
- 1 sweet potato (150 calories)

Afternoon Snack and Post Workout (around 180 calories)

- 1 scoop of whey protein (120 calories)
- 1 medium sized banana (60 calories)

Dinner (around 450 calories)

- 8 oz. 96% lean ground beef (350-400 calories)
- 3 servings vegetables (50-75 calories)

Evening Snack (around 270 calories)

- 1 serving steel cut oats (100-150 calories)
- ½ tbsp. Peanut butter (95-100 calories)
- 1 medium sized banana (60 calories)

Day 3

Breakfast (around 400 calories):

- 1 cup of oatmeal with flaxseed oil, 1 scoop of protein powder and blueberries. Mix everything into a bowl with water and microwave for 1-2 minutes.

Midmorning Snack (around 190 calories)

- 1 can of tuna (low sodium) (100 calories)
- 1 Greek Yogurt (fat free) (80-100 calories)

Lunch (around 480 calories)

- 1 Chicken breast sandwich with whole wheat bread, tomato, lettuce, and low-fat cheese (300 - 350 calories)
- 1 Cup of chili or black bean soup (180 calories)

Afternoon Snack and Post Workout (around 180 calories)

- 1 scoop of whey protein (120 calories)
- 1 medium sized banana (60 calories)

Dinner (around 600 calories)

- 10 oz. grilled salmon cooked in olive oil (400 - 450 calories)
- Side salad with romaine lettuce, pine nuts, carrots and balsamic vinaigrette (150 calories)
- 3 servings vegetables (50-75 calories)

Evening Snack (around 270 calories)

- 1 serving steel cut oats (100-150 calories)
- ½ tbsp. Peanut butter (95-100 calories)
- 1 medium sized banana (60 calories)

Supplements

A good workout routine and a clean diet are the most important steps on your way to a six-pack. They are necessary for building muscle and cannot be skipped. Supplements on the other hand, can enhance your diet, but won't do anything for you by themselves.

Protein Powder:

Protein powder is one of the few supplements that you should take year round. It helps you increase muscle repair/ growth and has no side effects (to a healthy adult). If you are new to bodybuilding you should test a few brands and see which one you like best. There is not much you can do wrong here.

Fat Burners

Due to their popularity and increased marketing, fat burners have become one of the most widely used supplements in bodybuilding. While there are some good fat burners, there are many you should avoid. Not necessarily because they will harm you, but simply because they are a waste of money. When buying a fat burner, you should always check the ingredients! Here is a list of the most common types of fat burners, their ingredients and how they affect your body. If you see something in you pre-workout that is not on the list, be sure to check for possible side effects:

Carb Blockers & Fat Blockers:

Carb blockers try to hinder the digestion of carbohydrates, which prevents your body from building up extra fat. This is usually done through white kidney bean extract, which binds to the carbohydrates you consume. Fat blockers work similarly through the use of chitosan. Instead of carbs they bind the the fat.

Thermogenic:

Thermogenic fat burners raise your internal body temperature through ingredients such as caffeine and yohimbe. This increases your resting heart rate, which leads to an increased metabolism.

Appetite Suppressants:

Good appetite suppressants use natural hoodia extract, which helps suppress your appetite and makes it easier to resist cravings.

Thyroid Regulators:

The thyroid is responsible for the regulation of your metabolism. A slow metabolism is often due to problems with the thyroid. If this is the case a thyroid regulator can be an option for you. The most important ingredients in thyroid regulators are guggulsterone and forskolin.

Green Tea (Extract)

Green tea extract is another popular ingredient. Due to its health benefits, however, it makes sense to add green tea extract to your diet even when not using any fat burners. Green tea helps fight off free radicals and toxins that attack body cells through cigarette smoke and UV sunlight. The caffeine in green tea also increases core temperature, resulting in more calories burned.

All Ab Exercises

The following list contains the best exercises for bigger and more defined abs. They are meant to give you an idea of how you can train your abs, should your old routine ever bore you. Every exercise is explained in detail with safety tips and possible variations.

Note: For the best exercises of all your muscle groups, check out my other book "The Gym Bible"

Ab Crunch

Main Muscle: Abdominals
Equipment: Body
Exercise Type: Isolation
Force: Pull

1. Position

Lie flat on your back with your feet resting on a bench with your knees bent at a 90-degree angle, or flat on the ground.

2. Execution

With hands lightly on either side of your head or neck, begin to roll your shoulders off the floor. They should come up off the floor only about 4 inches, while your lower back should remain on the floor. At the top of the motion, contract your abdominals hard and maintain the contraction for a second. Then, slowly lower to the original motion.

Tips & Safety

- Keep your lower back against the floor and your hips straight during the exercise.

- Focus on slow, controlled movement. Don't cheat yourself by swinging your upper body.

Variations

- There are hundreds of variations for the ab crunch. You can perform the exercise on top of an exercise ball or on a decline bench or with weights.

Ab Crunch with Legs on Stability Ball

Main Muscle: Abdominals
Equipment: Exercise Ball
Exercise Type: Isolation
Force: Pull

1. Position

Lie flat on your back with your feet resting on an exercise ball and your knees bent at a 90-degree angle. Position your feet around three inches apart and point both toes inward so they touch.

2. Execution

With hands positioned on either side of your head or neck, begin to roll your shoulders off the floor. They should come up off the floor only about four inches, while your lower back should remain on the floor. At the top of the motion, contract your abdominals hard and maintain the contraction for a second. Then, slowly lower to the initial position.

Tips & Safety

- Keep your lower back against the floor and your hips straight during the exercise.

- Focus on slow, controlled movement. Don't cheat yourself by swinging your upper body.

Variations

- Advanced lifters can hold a weighted plate in between hands for increase difficulty.

Stability Ball Ab Crunch

Main Muscle: Abdominals
Equipment: Exercise Ball
Exercise Type: Isolation
Force: Pull

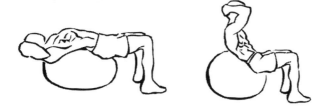

1. Position

Lie with your lower back pressed against the exercise ball and your feet pressed firmly against the floor. Make sure that your upper torso is hanging off the top of the ball. To avoid possible neck strains, you might want to cross your arms on top of your chest.

2. Execution

While exhaling, flex your waist by contracting the abdominals. Keep your neck stationary during this motion. At the top, contract your abdominals hard and maintain the contraction for a second. Then, slowly lower your upper body to the initial position while inhaling. Repeat.

Tips & Safety

- Make sure that your lower back always stays in contact with the ball.

- Focus on slow, controlled movement. Don't cheat yourself by swinging your upper body.

Variations

- You can also perform this exercise with a low pulley behind you with a rope attachment. The added resistance will increase the difficulty.

Main Muscle: Abdominals
Equipment: Exercise Ball
Exercise Type: Isolation
Force: Pull

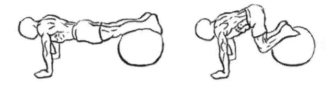

1. Position

Place your lower shins on top of an exercise ball and your hands on the floor in a push-up position around shoulder width apart. Fully extend your legs.

2. Execution

While exhaling, pull your knees in towards your chest. Keep your back completely straight as the ball rolls forward under your ankles. At the top, contract your abdominals hard and maintain the contraction for a second. While inhaling, slowly straighten your legs and let the ball roll back into the original position. Repeat.

Twisting Crunch / Cross Body Crunch

Main Muscle: Abdominals
Equipment: Body
Exercise Type: Compound
Force: Pull

1. Position

Lie flat on a mat. Position your hands behind head or neck.

2. Execution

Flex and twist your waist to raise your upper torso while bringing your left knee in toward your left shoulder at the same time. Reach with your elbow and try to touch your knee. Return until the backs of your shoulders touches the mat. Repeat on opposite side, alternating twists.

Tips & Safety

- While you cannot add weight to this exercise, you can concentrate on slow speed and perfect execution.

- Don't cheat yourself by jerking your upper body.

Variations

- You can also do all of your reps for one side and then switch to the other side.

Main Muscle: Abdominals

Equipment: Cable

Exercise Type: Isolation

Force: Pull

1. Position

Sit down on a flat bench with your back facing a high pulley. Position your hands over both shoulders and hold the cable rope attachment with both hands (palms should be facing each other).

2. Execution

While exhaling, flex the waist so the elbows travel toward the hips. Keep the hips stationary as you perform this step. While inhaling slowly return to the initial position. Repeat.

Tips & Safety

- When returning to the initial position, allow the weight to hyperextend your lower back slightly.

Variations

- You can also use exercise bands for this exercise.

- Cable crunches can also be done facing the high pulley.

Decline Crunch

Main Muscle: Abdominals
Equipment: Body
Exercise Type: Isolation
Force: Pull

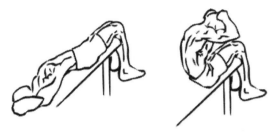

1. Position

Lie down on the decline bench and secure your legs at the end of the bench. Keeping your elbows in, position your hands lightly on either side of your head.

2. Execution

While exhaling and keeping your lower back on the bench, roll your shoulders off it. They should come up off the bench not more than five inches. Contract your abdominals hard at the top of the movement. While inhaling, slowly return to the starting position. Repeat.

Tips & Safety

- Do not lock your fingers behind your head.

- Do not swing your body and focus on slow movement.

Variations

- Advanced lifters can also add weight by holding a dumbbell on their chest.

Decline Cross Crunch

Main Muscle: Abdominals
Equipment: Body
Exercise Type: Compound
Force: Pull

1. Position

Lie down on the decline bench and secure your legs at the end of the bench. Position one hand beside your head and the other on your thigh.

2. Execution

While exhaling, raise your upper body off the bench while turning your torso to the left. Continue crunching up until your right elbow touches your opposite knee. While inhaling, slowly lower your body to the initial position. Repeat for recommended amount of repetitions and switch to other side.

Tips & Safety

- Try to keep your abs tight and the movement controlled and slow.

- Don't cheat yourself by swinging your upper body.

Variations

- You can also alternate from side to side in each repetition.

- You can also perform this exercise on a flat surface (see twisting crunch).

- Advanced lifters can also add weight by holding a dumbbell on their chest.

Leg Raise

Main Muscle: Abdominals
Equipment: Body
Exercise Type: Isolation
Force: Pull

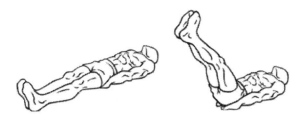

1. Position

Lie flat on a mat. Position your hands under your glutes with your palms down.

2. Execution

While exhaling and keeping your legs as straight as possible, raise your legs until they create a 90-degree angle with the floor. Hold the contraction at the top for a second. While inhaling, slowly lower your legs back down to the original position.

Tips & Safety

- Keep your lower back against the floor and your hips straight during the exercise.

- Focus on slow, controlled movement. Don't cheat yourself by swinging your legs.

Variations

- You can also perform this exercise on a bench with your legs hanging off.

- Advanced lifters can also add weight by holding a dumbbell in between their feet.

Bent Knee Hip Raise

Main Muscle: Abdominals
Equipment: Body
Exercise Type: Compound
Force: Pull

1. Position
Lie flat on a mat with your knee bent at around a 75-degree angle. Your arms should be right next to your sides. Now lift your feet off the floor by around two inches.

2. Execution
While exhaling, bring your knees in towards you as you keep your knees bent. Using only your lower abs, continue this movement and raise your hips off of the floor by rolling your pelvis backward (this part is not shown in the picture). Your knees should now be just above your chest. Contract your abs at the top of the movement and slowly return to the initial position slowly while inhaling.

Tips & Safety

- Focus on slow, controlled movement. Don't cheat yourself by swinging your legs.

Variations

- You can also straighten your feet or add ankle weights for increased difficulty.

Air Bike

Main Muscle: Abdominals
Equipment: Body
Exercise Type: Compound
Force: Pull

1. Position

Lie flat on a mat with your lower back pressed to the ground. Position your hands lightly on either side of your head and bring the knees up until your lower legs are parallel to the floor.

2. Execution

Simultaneously kick forward with the right leg and bring in the knee of the left leg. While exhaling, bring your right elbow close to your left knee by crunching to the side. The entire movement should simulate a cycle pedal motion. While inhaling, return to the initial position. Repeat the exercise with the opposite leg and continue alternating.

Tips & Safety

- Concentrate on perfect execution and slow speed.

- Keep your shoulder blades off the mat during the entire exercise.

Main Muscle: Abdominals
Equipment: Body
Exercise Type: Isolation
Force: Pull

1. Position
Using a slightly larger than shoulder width grip, hang from a chin-up bar with both arms extended at arms length. Your legs should be straight down and the pelvis rolled slightly backwards.

2. Execution
While exhaling, raise both legs until your torso makes a 90-degree angle with the legs. At the top, hold the contraction for a second. While inhaling, slowly lower your legs to the starting position.

Tips & Safety

- Perform the leg raise slowly and deliberately as it takes some getting used to.

- Don't cheat yourself by swinging your legs.

Variations

- For increased difficulty you can hold a dumbbell in between your feet.

- Hanging leg raises can also be performed using a vertical bench, which supports your upper back and allows you to place your elbows and arms on the side pads.

Main Muscle: Obliques

Secondary Muscle. Shoulders

Equipment: Body

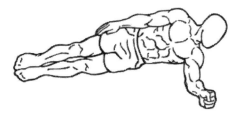

1. Position

Lie on one side and support your body between your forearm and knee to your feet.

2. Execution

While drawing your abs in, slowly raise your body so you are balanced on your feet and your forearm (see picture). Hold this position for about 30 - 60 seconds and slowly return back to the initial position. Switch sides and repeat.

Tips & Safety

- Do not let your waist sag. You will need to keep your upper body and legs straight while holding your own weight on your forearm.

- Gradually increase the time you hold the top position in future workout routines.

Ab Rollout

Main Muscle: Abdominals

Secondary Muscles: Deltoids, Lats, Lower Back

Equipment: Barbell

Exercise Type: Compound

Force: Pull

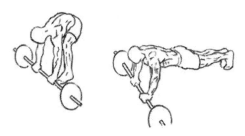

1. Position
Go into a pushup position and grab on to a barbell loaded with 5-10 lbs. on each side.

2. Execution
While exhaling, lift your hips and roll the barbell towards your feet. Remember to keep a slight arch on your back. Your arms should remain perpendicular to the floor throughout the movement. Otherwise, you will work out your back and shoulders more than the abs. Hold the contraction at the top for a second, then start to roll the barbell back and forward to the initial position slowly as you inhale.

Tips & Safety

- This exercise should not be done if you have back problems or difficulties maintaining stability.

- Keep your arms straight throughout the exercise.

Variations

- For less advanced athletes, this exercise can also be done on your knees (see next exercise).

Ab Rollout On Knees

Main Muscle: Abdominals

Secondary Muscles: Deltoids, Lats, Lower Back

Equipment: Barbell

Exercise Type: Compound

Force: Pull

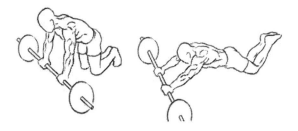

1. Position

Go into a pushup position with your knees on the floor and grab on to a barbell loaded with 5-10 lbs. on each side.

2. Execution

While exhaling, lift your hips and roll the barbell towards your knees. Remember to keep a slight arch on your back. Your arms should remain perpendicular to the floor throughout the movement. Otherwise, you will work out your back and shoulders more than the abs. Hold the contraction at the top for a second, then start to roll the barbell back and forward to the initial position slowly as you inhale.

Tips & Safety

- This exercise should not be done if you have back problems or difficulties maintaining stability.

- Keep your arms straight throughout the exercise.

Dumbbell Side Bends

Main Muscle: Abdominals
Equipment: Dumbbell
Exercise Type: Isolation
Force: Pull

1. Position

Stand up straight with a dumbbell in your right hand (palm facing the torso).
Your left hand should be holding your waist and your feet placed at shoulder
width.

2. Execution

While inhaling, bend at the waist to the right as far as possible. Keep your
head up and your back straight and during this movement. After holding for a
second, return to the initial position while exhaling. Repeat the movement on
the other side. Repeat for the recommended amount of repetitions and then
change hands.

Tips & Safety

- Only bend at the waist. Keep the rest of the body stationary!

Variations

- You can also do this exercise with a barbell or sitting on a bench.

Abdominal Draw In

Main Muscle: Abdominals
Equipment: Body
Exercise Type: Isolation
Force: Static

1. Position

Get down on a mat on your hands and knees, forming a square or four-point rectangle shape. Keep your hips and pelvis in a neutral position and your back straight.

2. Execution

Draw your abs in and crunch your abs while keeping your back still.
Hold for the contraction for around 20 seconds and then release. Returning to the initial position and repeat.

Tips & Safety

- Your back should be kept still all through out the contraction and relaxation.

- Once you get some practice, you can try holding the contraction for 40-60 seconds.

Variations

- You can also do this exercise standing up (feet shoulder width apart and hands on your hips).

If you enjoyed this book, please consider leaving a review on Amazon. Positive reviews help us authors out a lot and I would love to know what you thought about my work.

Sincerely
Felix Harder

Other Books By Felix Harder

Click On The Cover To Go To The Book

Made in the USA
Middletown, DE
22 April 2017